MASTER YOUR HEALTH WITH NUMEROLOGY

UNLOCK NUMERICAL INSIGHTS FOR WELL-BEING, OVERCOME DEPRESSION, ACTIVATE MIND-BODY HARMONY, AND REJUVENATE YOUR OVERALL LIFE FORCE

SOORAJ ACHAR
WWW.SOORAJ-ACHAR.COM

Copyright © 2023 by Sooraj Achar

All rights reserved.

No part of this book may be reproduced in any form without permission in writing from the author.

No part of this publication may be reproduced or transmitted in any form or by any means, mechanical or electronic, including photocopying or recording, or by any information storage and retrieval system, or transmitted by email or by any other means whatsoever without permission in writing from the author.

YOUR FREE GIFT !!

As a token of my thanks for taking out time to read my book, I would like to offer you a **Free-Gift**:

Scan Below **QR Code** to Download your **Free eBook PDF**.

Learn 395+ Surprising Psychology Words That Will Change The Way You Think - in the Next 30 Days!

You can also grab your **FREE GIFT** by typing in the below URL: **https://gift.sooraj-achar.com/**

ABOUT AUTHOR

Sooraj Achar, the Accomplished Author of "**Master Your HEALTH With Numerology**" - A Sensational **#1 Bestseller Across the Globe**

Dive into the world of **Sooraj Achar**, a prodigious author hailing from Bangalore, India, whose exceptional journey is as intriguing as the profound concepts explored in his works. With "Master Your HEALTH With Numerology," Sooraj has transcended borders, achieving the coveted status of **#1 Bestseller** in the United States, the United Kingdom, Canada, India, and Australia.

A Remarkable Beginnings:

Sooraj Achar's extraordinary odyssey commenced in the vibrant city of Bangalore, India. As a young dreamer, his fascination with mathematics sparked an early connection with the enigmatic world of numbers. This infatuation, initially drawn from captivating numerological stories, sowed the seeds for a lifetime dedicated to the exploration of **Numerical Mysteries**.

A Multifaceted Expert:

Today, **Sooraj Achar** stands as not just an accomplished Software Engineer but also a passionate connoisseur of **numerology** and the ancient science of **Feng-Shui (Vastu)**. His multifaceted persona extends to **coaching and consulting**, where he delves into the profound questions of Health, Relationships, Careers, and Money (HRCM). Sooraj is a certified **Ho'oponopono & EFT Healer and NLP Practitioner**, renowned for his transformative abilities in bringing about balance, harmony, and fulfillment in the lives of countless individuals.

A Seeker of Wisdom:

Sooraj's relentless quest for knowledge has led him to the intricate realms of human psychology and behavior. His dedication to understanding the human psyche and optimizing life's potential is unwavering. As a perpetual learner, he embodies the principles of optimal living and shares his wisdom to empower others to lead resourceful lives.

A Believer in Unlimited Potential:

Above all, **Sooraj Achar** is a firm believer in the limitless potential residing within each individual. He ardently champions the idea that every person possesses the capacity to achieve far beyond their self-imposed limits. Through his words and wisdom, he inspires others to unlock their hidden potential and lead lives of purpose and abundance.

For more life-altering insights, delve into Sooraj Achar's remarkable catalog of books. Visit www.sooraj-achar.com and embark on a journey of self-discovery and transformation.

Stay Connected:

Explore the latest updates, thought-provoking content, and inspiring messages from Sooraj Achar by connecting with him through our social media channels. Join us in the pursuit of a fulfilling and harmonious life.

https://amzn.to/3CgQHF9

https://medium.com/@soorajachar99

https://bit.ly/3M7gIu2

instagram.com/psychology_of_numberz/

https://bit.ly/3dO6aDh

MASTER YOUR HEALTH WITH NUMEROLOGY

https://bit.ly/3LXBTyz

https://bit.ly/3E9vKxc

ACKNOWLEDGMENT

How does a person say "**Thank You**" when there are so many people to thank?

Obviously, this book is a big thank you to my father **G Sathyanarayan Achar,** who is a powerful role model, and my mother **G Pramila,** who taught me love and kindness.

I extend my heartfelt appreciation to my sister, **Shruthi S**, brother-in-law, **Saravana P**, and adorable niece, **Naveeksha S**, who have played pivotal roles in making this book a reality. Their presence makes my life complete.

A special acknowledgment is reserved for my mentor, **Mr. Arvind Sood**, whose guidance led me to become a **Numerology and Vaastu Coach**

and Consultant. I am privileged to have received permission to use the term "Driver-Conductor," a creation of Mr. Arvind Sood.

I owe thanks to **Mr. Som Bathla**, an **Amazon #1 Bestselling** author, for his mentorship, motivation, and guidance in the realms of **Writing, Self-Publishing, and Launching Books**. His support has been instrumental in initiating my journey as an Authorpreneur.

Finally, heartfelt gratitude to my dedicated team – **Avesh Ansari**, **Akshay Bhat**, and **Md. Bilal** – for their unwavering support and contributions.

DEDICATION

This Book is Dedicated to My Grandparents,

R. Gangadhar & G. Vishalakshamma

And, My Dear Brother **Arvind Achar.**

FOREWORD

1. Prof. Wg Cdr Dr. S.P. Kaushik

Dear Reader,

It is with great pleasure that I introduce the insightful book "Master Your Destiny with Numerology" by Sooraj Achar. In this enlightening read, Sooraj delves into the mystique of numerology, unraveling its profound significance in our lives.

As you embark on the journey of this book, you will discover the magical power hidden within your true potential. Sooraj brilliantly navigates through the world of numbers, explaining the intricate role they play in shaping our destinies. With a keen eye and deep understanding, he explores the nuances of numerology, demystifying questions that have intrigued many.

The beauty of this book lies in its simplicity. Sooraj has effortlessly translated complex concepts into everyday language, making the wisdom of numerology accessible to all. By understanding the significance of your date of birth, you can unlock the secrets to your strengths and weaknesses, empowering yourself to overcome challenges and embrace success.

Numerology, as Sooraj passionately asserts, is not mere superstition; it is a science, a guiding force that can transform your life. By following the principles outlined in this book, you can harness the miraculous potential within you. Sooraj's insights will not only inspire you but also provide practical tools to navigate life's journey with confidence and grace.

I wholeheartedly recommend this book to anyone seeking self-discovery, personal growth, and a deeper understanding of the profound impact numbers have on our lives. May this book be your guiding light, illuminating the path to a future filled with success, happiness, and fulfillment.

Warm regards,
Prof. Wg Cdr Dr. S.P. Kaushik
Former Director General & Pro Vice-Chancellor

2. K. Vikram Rastogi

This Book Inspires A Life Transformation

It is with great pleasure and enthusiasm that I introduce you to "Master Your Destiny with Numerology" by the prolific author, Sooraj Achar. I have had the privilege of knowing him personally for several years, and his dedication to the field of numerology is nothing short of inspiring. Through his 10 bestselling books, Sooraj has enlightened countless individuals on the incredible potential of numerology, and with this latest addition to his literary journey, he delves deeper into the intricacies of this ancient science to empower you to take control of your life.

As far as I am concerned, numerology had a profound impact on my life since the tender age of 18 when I had an opportunity to read the book on Numerology by Cheiro. It inspired me to acquire the admirable qualities of Abraham Lincoln and Charles Darwin, who shared my birthdate. Over the next 60 years, this influence played a significant role in shaping my character and life journey.

In today's world, where the hustle and bustle of life often distract us from the profound mysteries that surround us, numerology stands as a beacon of light. It is a testament to the fundamental truth that our lives are not mere coincidences but intricate patterns woven into the fabric of the universe. The importance of numerology cannot be understated. We have seen glimpses of this wisdom in earlier works like Cheiro's, among others, but Sooraj Achar takes us on a journey that uncovers the profound influence of numbers on our destiny.

"Master Your Destiny with Numerology" is a treasure trove of insights and revelations. Sooraj's mastery of presenting complex concepts in a simple and relatable manner shines through this book. He seamlessly weaves together the theoretical foundation of numerology with practical applications. The salient features of this book are that it contains numerous case studies that bring the subject to life. These real-life examples demonstrate how numerology can be applied to diverse aspects of our lives, including wealth, health, career, happiness, and general well-being.

Many of us often wonder how we can shape our own destiny. "Master Your Destiny with Numerology" holds the key to answering this age-old question. Through the exploration of numbers and their significance, Sooraj shows us that we have the power to influence the course of our lives. This book is not just a guide but a roadmap to understanding the intricate relationship between numbers and our personal journey. It offers practical tools and methods to align your life with the positive energies that numerology unveils.

However, it is essential to approach numerology with caution and diligence. The power of numbers is immense, and as Sooraj Achar emphasizes, the precautions to be taken for implementing the recommendations derived from numerology are critical. Numerology can reveal the hidden dynamics of our lives, but it should be approached with respect and responsibility. This book provides valuable insights on how to harness the potential of numerology without succumbing to its pitfalls.

In conclusion, "Master Your Destiny with Numerology" is a testament to Sooraj Achar's dedication to helping individuals uncover the profound wisdom that numerology holds. His work benefits not only individuals but also society at large. As we master our own destinies, we contribute to the betterment of humanity. Sooraj's teachings go beyond personal enrichment; they extend to the betterment of citizens and ultimately our entire country.

In the pages that follow, you will embark on a journey of self-discovery and empowerment. Sooraj Achar's wisdom, backed by his extensive experience and knowledge in numerology, will be your guiding light. As you delve into the depths of this book, I hope you find the answers you seek, not only for your own life but for the benefit of all human beings, citizens, and our great nation. "Master Your Destiny with Numerology" is not just a book; it is a powerful tool that has the potential to transform lives and shape destinies for the better. Enjoy the journey, and may you master your destiny with the profound wisdom of numerology.

K. Vikram Rastogi
Co-author of Secrets of Happy Healthy Long Life

3. KR Goswami

In the symphony of life, where the intricate notes of destiny intertwine with our choices, I stumbled upon a revelation that altered the very fabric of my existence—the profound wisdom of Numerology. It was not just any exploration, but an odyssey illuminated by the brilliance of Sooraj Achar's literary masterpiece, "Life Mastery Using Numerology."

Sooraj's narrative transcends the conventional, unlocking the celestial code that governs our destinies. The resonance of his insights echoed through the corridors of my life, transforming my understanding of Numerology from mere theory to a potent force for change. I found myself entwined with the rhythm of his words, orchestrating a symphony of transformation that extended far beyond the pages of his book.

Recently, as I embarked on the journey of aligning the energies of my newly acquired abode in Ahmedabad through Vastu, Sooraj's teachings became my guiding compass. His principles, gleaned from a profound comprehension of Numerology, manifested as an anchor amidst the swirling currents of change. Through his literary prowess, he not only imparts wisdom but also extends a helping hand to fledgling writers, nurturing the flame of creativity within them.

Sooraj Achar, a luminary in the realm of literature, is not just an author of best-selling books but a mentor and guide, selflessly fostering the growth of aspiring wordsmiths. His benevolence extends beyond the confines of his written works, as he shares the wealth of his expert knowledge with an open heart.

As a retired defense personnel akin to his father, I resonate with Sooraj's humility and soft-spoken demeanor. His words transcend the boundaries of the page, creating a bridge that connects our shared experiences and aspirations. Through his books, I discovered a mentor who not only enlightens but also uplifts—a beacon of inspiration in the vast sea of knowledge.

From the vantage point of a psychologist, I delved into the rich tapestry of Sooraj's Numerology series, captivated by the intricate dance of numbers and psychology. As a banker, immersed in the world of numbers and intricate calculations, I found solace and resonance in the harmonious blend of logic and mysticism that permeates his writings.

The transformative impact of Sooraj's Numerology books reverberates across every facet of my life, especially in the realm of relationships. It has been the cornerstone of forging unbreakable bonds with family, friends, and associates—a testament to the universality and applicability of his teachings.

Sooraj, as you embark on the journey of yet another literary masterpiece, I extend my heartfelt wishes for the success of the intellectual gems you've crafted. May your words continue to resonate across borders, shaping the intellectual landscape with international acclaim.

In gratitude and admiration,

KR Goswami

Former Aircraft Engineer, Retired Branch Manager SBI, Psychologist, Best-selling Author, and Defence recruitment trainer

4. Dr. Arundhati Govind Hoskeri

Man's fascination with numbers is unique; it seems humans might have delved into counting even before mastering the art of speech! Numerology, a discipline that explores the mystical connections between life events and numbers, has been a global practice for centuries. This study carefully examines the numerical values assigned to letters, words, and names through alphanumeric systems.

It's heartening to see a growing interest among educated youth in this divinatory art and science of Numerology. Sooraj Achar, a Software Engineer, has immersed himself deeply in the study of

Numerology and is now generously sharing his knowledge with others.

In his latest book, "Master Your Destiny With Numerology," Sooraj not only imparts fundamental knowledge accessible to a layman but also provides a comprehensive, step-by-step guide to help readers carve their paths toward desired goals and success.

The book seamlessly integrates Eastern and Western perspectives on number divination, delving into the influence of planets associated with each number and their vibrations on individuals. Sooraj offers corrective measures to strengthen these vibrations, facilitating the achievement of desired results.

An intriguing aspect of the book is Sooraj's exploration of a 4000-year-old Chinese Numerology known as the "Lo Shu Grid," presented in a manner that is easy to study and comprehend.

Readers will discover their Destiny Numbers and Life Path Numbers and learn to resonate positively with their names, phone numbers, cars, lottery tickets, journeys, and practically everything else.

Sooraj's meticulous research and profound understanding of the subject are evident throughout the book. I'm confident that readers will greatly benefit from his wealth of knowledge. I wish Sooraj Achar all the very best for this exciting new venture!

Dr Arundhati Govind Hoskeri
MSc, MEd, MA (English Literature), PhD, ACTL Diploma in Public Speaking (Trinity College of London), NDHS(Doctor of Natural Health Sciences)
Educational Consultant for Cambridge International Schools
Former Director and Principal of Cambridge International School and I B World School

5. Dr. P. NEELA

"MASTER YOUR DESTINY WITH NUMEROLOGY" by Sooraj Achar

Numerology is the ancient study of numbers and their meanings. It has been used for centuries to understand the human personality, predict the future, and make better decisions in life.

In his book, "MASTER YOUR DESTINY WITH NUMEROLOGY," Sooraj Achar provides a comprehensive and practical guide to using numerology to transform your life. He covers all basic and essential aspects of numerology, including:

- How to calculate your life path number, destiny number, soul urge number, and personality number

- What does each number mean and how

does it influence your life

- How to use numerology to find your strengths and weaknesses, identify your life purpose, and make better choices

- How to use numerology to improve your relationships, finances, and overall well-being

Achar also provides a number of simple and effective remedies that you can use to address any challenges you may be facing in your life.

Whether you are a beginner or an experienced numerologist, "MASTER YOUR DESTINY WITH NUMEROLOGY" is an essential resource for anyone who wants to use the power of numbers to create the life they desire.

Some specific benefits that you can expect to gain from reading this book include personal transformation harmonious relationships, financial abundance, self-discovery, etc,

If you are ready to take control of your destiny and create the life you desire, then "MASTER YOUR DESTINY WITH NUMEROLOGY" is the book for you. Sooraj Achar provides a clear and concise guide to using numerology to transform your life in all areas. I wish you all success!!!

**Dr. P. NEELA
Josh Talks Speaker**

CONTENTS

How This Book Can Work Miracles in Your Life? — XXXII

Chapter Highlights: Top 5 Takeaways And Insights — XXXVII

IMPORTANT! - Before You Proceed — LVI

1. A Guide to Identifying Your Health Sector — 1

2. Recognizing Depression and Strategies for Healing — 5

3. Why Do You Frequently Fall Ill? Detect and Uplift Your Health Sector — 9

4. Identifying Spiritual Progress and Divine Connections through Your Birthdate — 14

5. Elevating Your Wellness, Wealth, and Relationship Domains — 17

6. Numerology's Universal Remedy: A Master Solution for All Challenges — 21

7. The Significance of February 5th: Commencement of the Personal Year — 26

8. Adjusting Fate: Remedies for Changes in Personal Year — 32

9. A Deep Dive into Direct and Indirect Solutions — 35

10. Numerology's Insight into Children's Social Circles: Identifying Risks — 41

11. Navigating Time: Choosing the Right Wrist Companion — 44

12. Choosing the Right Pendant: A Guide for Challenging Birth Dates — 47

Conclusion — 53

May I Ask You For A Small Favor? — 55

Preview of My Next Book in the Series — 57

Preview of My Best Selling Books	60
Testimonials	78
Author Profile	85
Disclaimer	88

HOW THIS BOOK CAN WORK MIRACLES IN YOUR LIFE?

"Numbers hold the keys to the kingdom of health. Mastering your well-being through numerology is not just a choice; it's a calculated step toward a healthier life."

In the pursuit of holistic well-being, "Master Your HEALTH With Numerology" is not just a book—it's a transformative guide that can work miracles in your life. This unique exploration into the realm of health and numerology unveils a path to optimal well-being, inviting you to discover the profound connections between your numerical code and the vitality of your mind and body.

How This Book Can Work Miracles in Your Life

1. Unlock Numerical Insights:

Dive deep into the world of numerology to unlock hidden insights about your health. This book serves as a key to deciphering the numerical codes that influence your overall well-being.

2. Optimal Well-being Unveiled:

Explore the correlation between your numerology and your health, uncovering the secrets to achieving optimal well-being. This book guides you toward a state of balance and vitality.

3. Mind-Body Harmony:

Understand the intricate connection between your mind and body through the lens of numerology. Achieve harmony by aligning your mental and physical well-being with the numerical forces at play.

4. Overcome Depression:

Delve into transformative insights that can aid in overcoming depression. This book offers a holistic approach, incorporating numerological wisdom to help lift the clouds of despair and usher in a brighter mental landscape.

5. Rejuvenate Your Life Force:

Tap into the rejuvenating power of numerology to invigorate your life force. Discover practices and perspectives that breathe new life into your existence, fostering vitality and longevity.

6. Personalized Wellness Strategies:

This book provides personalized strategies for wellness based on your unique numerological profile. Tailor your health journey according to the specific needs illuminated by your numerical code.

7. Navigate Numerical Influences:

Life is a tapestry woven with numerical influences. Learn how to navigate these forces to enhance your health. This book empowers you to make informed choices that align with your numerological strengths.

8. Transformative Practices:

Immerse yourself in transformative practices designed to elevate your health. From dietary choices to mindfulness techniques, this book integrates numerological insights into actionable steps for a healthier lifestyle.

9. Elevate Mental Resilience:

Numerology plays a role in shaping your mental resilience. Explore how understanding your numerical code can empower you to face challenges with a strengthened and resilient mindset.

10. Numerology as a Healing Tool:

This book introduces numerology not just as a system of understanding, but as a healing tool. Witness how embracing the numerical aspects of your life can initiate profound healing and wellness.

11. Decode Physical Ailments:

Uncover the symbolic language of numerology to decode potential root causes of physical ailments. This book guides you in addressing health issues at a foundational level.

12. Embrace Vibrant Living:

Shift from mere existence to vibrant living as you incorporate the teachings of this book. Witness the miracles unfold as you align with the numerological currents guiding your path.

"Master Your HEALTH With Numerology" is a transformative journey that extends beyond the pages. It is an invitation to witness the miracles that can manifest when you intertwine the wisdom of numerology with your pursuit of optimal health. Embrace the revelations within, and let the miracles unfold in your life's journey to profound well-being.

CHAPTER HIGHLIGHTS: TOP 5 TAKEAWAYS AND INSIGHTS

1. Key Takeaways for the Chapter - A Guide To Identifying Your Health Sector

1. Number 7 and Health: The presence of the number 7 in the birth chart signals the health sector. One 7 suggests minor health issues, while multiple 7s can indicate persistent health problems.

2. Impact of Kua Numbers: Multiple sevens originating from the Kua number have a less significant impact on health. Kua numbers alone are not potent enough to strongly influence health.

3. No 7, Good Health: Absence of the number 7 generally indicates good health. Individuals without the number 7 in their birth chart are expected to maintain good health throughout their lives.

4. D-C Combination and Health: An anti or opposite D-C combination with multiple 7s represents a worst-case scenario, indicating very weak health. The D-C combination plays a crucial role in determining health conditions.

5. Name Spelling and Health: Even with a favorable D-C combination and no 7 in the chart, health issues may arise if the name spelling is anti with the Driver. Correct name spelling and compatibility with the date of birth are essential for maintaining good health.

2. Key Takeaways for the Chapter - Recognizing Depression And Strategies For Healing

1. Depression Factors: Multiple occurrences of the number 2 (Moon), unfavorable D-C combinations,

and specific personal years, such as 9 or those anti to the Driver, can contribute to a higher likelihood of depression.

2. Moon and Rahu Combination: A D-C combination where the driver is 4 and the conductor is 2, or vice versa, indicates the Moon in the company of Rahu, resembling a queen with a gangster. This combination may lead to depression due to a preference for isolation.

3. Personal Year Impact: A personal year of 9 or one that is anti to the Driver, combined with other depression indicators in the birth chart, increases the chances of experiencing depression during that year.

4. Chart and D-C Influence: Multiple occurrences of the number 2 and an anti-D-C combination intensify the inclination towards depression. Understanding these aspects helps identify individuals prone to depressive episodes.

5. Solutions and Remedies: While the birth chart and D-C combination may not change, mental and

emotional support, especially from parents, proves crucial. Spending quality time, communication, vacations, and play can positively impact individuals with depression indicators. Remedies like Gayatri Yantra and Crystal bracelets are recommended for additional support.

3. Key Takeaways for the Chapter – Why Do You Frequently Fall Ill? Detect And Uplift Your Health Sector

1. Numerology for Health: Utilize numerology to gain insights into health issues. Explore specific yogas and remedies based on your date of birth for maintaining well-being.

2. Driver and Conductor Analysis: Identify your driver and conductor numbers by summing the digits of your date of birth. Incompatibility or opposition between these numbers signals potential health challenges.

3. Yogas for Health Issues: Examine driver-conductor combinations like 1/8, 8/1, 4/9,

9/4, 2/8, 8/2, and 2/6, as they indicate yogas associated with health problems.

4. Multiple Sevens Impact: Presence of multiple sevens in your chart may contribute to health struggles. Evaluate the impact of this number on your overall well-being.

5. Name Spelling Significance: The spelling of your name, especially if it opposes your driver or conductor, can influence health. Correcting the name spelling is a practical step to enhance your health sector.

4. Key Takeaways for the Chapter – Identifying Spiritual Progress And Divine Connections Through Your Birthdate

1. Spiritual Indicators: Numerology reveals that Jupiter (3) and Ketu (7) are key planetary numbers pointing towards a spiritual journey. Ketu, being more potent, holds greater significance in indicating a profound connection to spirituality.

2. Catalyst for Spirituality: While both Jupiter and Ketu contribute to spiritual growth, Jupiter acts as a catalyst, enhancing the spiritual inclination signaled by Ketu. Even possessing the number 3 alone can influence a spiritual journey.

3. Direct Presence in DOB or Chart: For a significant impact, numbers 3 and 7 should be directly present in your date of birth (DOB) or appear as driver or conductor numbers in your numerology chart.

4. Caution with Number 6: Conflict may arise if the chart includes numbers 3, 7, and 6 simultaneously. While 3 and 7 encourage spirituality, 6 leans towards a luxurious lifestyle, creating a potential conflict in life choices.

5. Illustrative Example: The provided date of birth (13-02-1967) demonstrates the potential conflict, where D=4, C=2, and K=6, offering a practical illustration of the discussed numerological dynamics.

5. Key Takeaways for the Chapter – Elevating Your Wellness, Wealth, And Relationship Domains

1. Essential Life Aspects: The chapter emphasizes the paramount importance of health, money, relationships, and often-overlooked spiritualism in an individual's life journey from birth to death.

2. Money and Career Zones: North and west zones are highlighted for financial prosperity, with the north associated with Kuber and the west linked to Varun, the father of Goddess Laxmi. Keeping these zones clutter-free is advised for sustained career success.

3. Financial Utilization: The southeast (S-E) zone, governed by Venus, is indirectly tied to money, luxury, and glamour. Maintaining a defect-free SE zone is crucial for optimal financial utilization and avoiding unnecessary expenses.

4. Health Mastery Zones: North-east and east zones are identified as the master zones for health. A

clean, well-ventilated environment in these areas is recommended to prevent head-related problems and enhance overall well-being.

5. Relationship-Focused Zones: East is designated as the zone for family relations, while south and south-west are crucial for commercial relations. Defect-free zones and precautions against T-points and underground water bodies are advised for fostering strong relationships. Additionally, the often-overlooked aspect of spiritualism is connected to the North-East and East zones.

6. Key Takeaways for the Chapter – Numerology's Universal Remedy: A Master Solution For All Challenges

1. Master Solution Concept: The chapter introduces the concept of a 'master solution,' distinct from remedies, as an effective approach to challenges in one's date of birth.

2. Dependable Lord Ganesh: When facing confusion, loss of control, or despair, the chapter

recommends seeking refuge under Lord Ganesh. This master solution is portrayed as reliable, even when other remedies seem ineffective.

3. Offerings and Prayer: On Mondays or Wednesdays, the suggested ritual involves offering bundi or besan laddus, a yellow scarf, and a modest 5 or 10 rupee coin to Lord Ganesh. While making these offerings, one is encouraged to pray for problem resolution.

4. Visualization Technique: The chapter introduces a visualization technique where individuals should close their eyes, focus on Lord Ganesh, and imagine the problem being solved. Envisioning a happy life without the problem is a crucial aspect of this process.

5. Power of Prayer: Emphasizing the potency of prayers, the chapter concludes by asserting that prayers hold greater power than any other solution, highlighting the significance of a spiritual approach in overcoming life's challenges.

7. Key Takeaways for the Chapter – The Significance Of February 5th: Commencement Of The Personal Year

1. Significance of Personal Years, Months, and Days: The chapter underscores the importance of personal years, months, and days in guiding life decisions, helping to navigate challenges, and planning for the future.

2. Personal Year Calculation: It provides a step-by-step guide for calculating the personal year, emphasizing the importance of comparing it with the driver number to gauge the year's overall impact.

3. Personal Month Calculation: Explains the calculation of personal months, highlighting how it influences decision-making in specific months. The relationship with the driver number is crucial in determining the month's impact.

4. Personal Day Calculation: Details the process of calculating personal days, emphasizing the addition of personal year, personal month, and day total.

The resulting number guides decision-making on specific days, considering its compatibility with the driver number.

5. Starting a Personal Year: Distinguishes between a new year and a personal year, noting that a personal year begins on the 5th of February. Stresses the dominance of the personal year in influencing the overall yearly experiences, with additional consideration of personal months and days for significant decisions.

8. Key Takeaways for the Chapter – Adjusting Fate: Remedies For Changes In Personal Year

1. Consistency in Remedies: Emphasizes that remedies chosen based on date of birth and astrological charts do not need yearly adjustments. Changing remedies annually is unnecessary as the personal year's influence is temporary and does not impact the efficacy of chosen remedies.

2. Personal Year-Remedy Relationship: Clarifies that personal year numbers do not affect astrological charts or remedies. The personal year merely indicates the behavioral aspects of a particular year, and remedies remain consistent based on individual needs and missing numbers.

3. Temporary Nature of Personal Year: Highlights that the relationship between the personal year and the driver number is temporary. Temporary relations, such as personal year influences, do not significantly impact overall fortune.

4. Effectiveness of Remedies: Warns against frequent changes to selected remedies, stating that constant adjustments diminish their effectiveness. Consistency in following chosen remedies is key for their long-term impact.

5. Special Consideration for Personal Year 9 or Anti-Driver: Recommends acquiring Gayatri Yantra during a personal year of 9 or when it is anti to the driver. Gayatri Yantra is suggested to manage this period effectively, eliminating the need for changes in existing remedies.

9. Key Takeaways for the Chapter – A Deep Dive Into Direct And Indirect Solutions

1. Direct vs. Indirect Remedies: Explains the difference between direct and indirect remedies based on the compatibility of the driver and conductor numbers. Direct remedies are chosen when the D-C combination is neutral or friendly, while indirect remedies are considered for opposite combinations.

2. Example A - Opposite Combination: Illustrates with an example where the driver and conductor numbers are opposite, making direct remedies unsuitable. Describes the process of selecting remedies for missing numbers (5 and 8) that are compatible with the driver.

3. Example B - Anti Combination: Demonstrates a scenario where the D-C combination is anti, prohibiting direct remedies for the driver and conductor. Guides the selection of indirect

remedies for missing numbers (2, 4, 3, 7, 6) based on compatibility.

4. Example C - Friend Combination: Highlights a case with a friendly D-C combination, allowing for direct remedies. Guides the selection of direct and indirect remedies for missing numbers (4, 3, 2) based on their compatibility with the driver and conductor.

5. Indirect Remedies Overview: Lists specific indirect remedies for missing numbers, including wearing crystal bracelets, applying red tilak for number 9, offering water to the sun for number 1, and wearing specific metal strap watches for numbers 7 and 6. Emphasizes that Kua number is not relevant in remedy selection.

10. Key Takeaways for the Chapter – Numerology's Insight Into Children's Social Circles: Identifying Risks

1. Identifying Bad Company Numbers: Highlights the significance of a child's date of birth (DOB) in

determining the likelihood of getting involved in bad company. Numbers 4, 2, and 8 are associated with this inclination, emphasizing the influence of the environment on a child with these numbers.

2. Caution with DC Combinations: Warns against specific D-C combinations, such as 6-6, 4-8, 4-4, or 1-1, which may increase the chances of a child getting involved in bad company. Encourages parents to be vigilant and understand the potential impact of these combinations on their child's behavior.

3. Obedience Linked to Number 6: Discusses the role of the number 6 as a key factor in predicting a child's obedience. Emphasizes that having 6 in the birth chart, excluding the Kua number, significantly increases the likelihood of the child being obedient.

4. Environmental Influence: Stresses the impact of the child's environment on behavioral traits. Acknowledges that while numbers indicate tendencies, creating a positive and nurturing environment is crucial for a child's development and behavior.

5. Complimentary Number 5 for Obedience: Notes that in the absence of the number 6, its complimentary number 5 can contribute to a child's obedience. Encourages parents to foster a supportive environment and consider these numerical insights as part of a holistic approach to parenting.

11. Key Takeaways for the Chapter – Navigating Time: Choosing The Right Wrist Companion

1. Significance of Wearing Wristwatches: Explores the importance of wearing wristwatches despite the prevalence of mobile phones. Emphasizes the positive impact on fortune, drawing attention to the numerological perspective.

2. Left or Right Hand Option: Addresses the common practice of wearing watches on the left hand but assures that wearing it on the right hand is acceptable. Provides flexibility in personal preference.

3. Preferred Material – Metal Strap/Chain: Recommends opting for watches with metal straps or chains over leather and rubber. Highlights the energetic benefits of metal, fostering energy transfer and positively influencing energy levels.

4. Color Considerations: Advises on the color of the watch chain/strap, favoring golden or a mix of golden and silver. Discourages wearing silver color alone, providing insights into the numerological significance of colors.

5. Watches as Living Energy: Conceptualizes watches as living things due to their energy source and moving parts. Explains the rationale behind avoiding leather and rubber straps, promoting the flow of energy into the body through metal straps, enhancing energy levels, and positively impacting opportunity and relationship sectors.

12. Key Takeaways for the Chapter - Choosing The Right Pendant: A Guide For Challenging Birth Dates

1. Challenges with Tricky DOBs: Addresses complexities in numerology calculations arising from tricky dates of birth, offering practical examples to guide appropriate yantra selection.

2. Yantra Selection for Absent Numbers: Illustrates the significance of yantras for missing numbers in a chart, emphasizing the importance of choosing the right yantra by considering both the driver and conductor numbers.

3. Case-specific Yantra Recommendations: Provides specific examples, advising the selection of yantras based on the unique characteristics of each date of birth, ensuring compatibility with driver and conductor numbers.

4. Maintenance and Authenticity of Yantras: Stresses the importance of maintaining yantras made of silver, cautioning against corrosion that

diminishes their power. Emphasizes authenticity and the need for new yantras, personalized for individual energy.

5. Yantras vs. Gemstones: Debunks the significance of gemstones in numerology, advocating for yantras due to their authenticity, affordability, and ease of use. Discusses the ineffectiveness and questionable authenticity of gemstones compared to the pure and powerful nature of yantras.

6. Role of Yantras and Bracelets: Highlights the efficacy and affordability of yantras over gemstones, focusing on their authenticity and connection to ancient shastras. Suggests bracelets as an effective and convenient alternative for numerological remedies, offering flexibility based on individual needs and missing numbers.

IMPORTANT! - BEFORE YOU PROCEED

Important Note to Readers

Dear Reader,

Before embarking on the insightful journey presented in this book, "Master Your MONEY With Numerology," we highly recommend delving into the foundational knowledge provided in the first six chapters of the Numerology Mastery series – "Master Your DESTINY With Numerology." These initial chapters serve as the cornerstone for understanding the core principles and concepts that underpin the world of numerology.

In "Master Your DESTINY With Numerology," we unravel the mysteries of numerology, exploring the profound connections between your date of birth and the intricate tapestry of your life. The insights gained from these foundational chapters will lay a robust groundwork for comprehending the advanced concepts and applications discussed in this present volume.

Kindly Download Your "Free Book" By Scanning the QR Code or Clicking the Link Below:

"FREE MASTERY BOOK"

The mastery of numerology is a progressive journey, much like building a house where a sturdy foundation ensures the strength and stability of the entire structure. Likewise, the knowledge gained from the initial chapters acts as the bedrock, enhancing your ability to grasp the intricacies of financial empowerment explored in "Master Your MONEY With Numerology."

By familiarizing yourself with the foundational principles, you'll be better equipped to extract maximum value from the advanced techniques, personalized analyzes, and strategic insights presented in subsequent chapters. We encourage you to absorb the wisdom shared in the earlier segments to fully harness the transformative potential that numerology offers on your path to financial mastery.

Thank you for your commitment to self-discovery and empowerment through numerology.

Wishing you an enriching and enlightening reading experience.

Warm regards,
Sooraj Achar
Author, Numerology Mastery Series

Chapter 1
A Guide to Identifying Your Health Sector

"In the intricate dance of numbers, your health unfolds its secrets. Master your health with the wisdom of numerology, where every digit tells a tale of well-being."

In the vast landscape of health, understanding your specific sector is paramount. This chapter serves as a guide, unraveling the intricacies of identifying and navigating your unique path within the diverse realm of healthcare.

How can we tell about one's health sector based on their date of birth? What are the points to determine a health sector? Let's know in this chapter.

There are some point about the health sector:

- Number 7, which represents Ketu, is responsible for the health sector. If the number 7 appears only once in someone's birth chart, it won't have a significant impact on their health; there might be some minor health problems. However, if there are two 7s in the chart, the person's health is likely to be weak. And if there are more than two 7s, the person may experience persistent health issues. They might find themselves constantly consulting doctors, undergoing diagnostic tests, and taking medications.

- If multiple sevens originate from the Kua number, they won't exert a substantial influence. Kua numbers are not potent enough to make a significant impact.

- If there is no 7 in a person's birth chart, their health is expected to remain in good condition throughout their life.

- If the D-C combination is anti or opposite when there are multiple 7s in the chart, it represents the worst possible condition. This person's health will be very weak.

- Even if the number 7 is absent in the chart, when the Driver is 1 and the Conductor is 8, there is a high likelihood of poor health.

- If one has a favorable D-C combination and no 7 in the chart, there is still a possibility of health issues if the name spelling is anti with the Driver. For example, if the Driver is 1 and the name spelling is associated with 8, it indicates a potential for poor health.

If you have multiple sevens or anti/opposite D-C combinations, you need to follow the remedies that we have discussed before. Gayatri Pendent is super helpful in these cases. At Least you should make sure that your name spelling is correct and compatible with your DOB.

Chapter 2

Recognizing Depression and Strategies for Healing

"Unlock the numerical code to vibrant living. Numerology isn't just about numbers; it's a guide to mastering your health, aligning your energies, and embracing well-being."

Do you know by examining our DOB, driver, conductor, and Lo Shu grid we can gain unique insights into the days of our lives when we may encounter feelings of depression or emotional challenges? Let's discuss this in this chapter.

Factors of Depression:

    1. 2= Moon

    2. D-C Combination

    3. Your personal year

Now let's understand with some examples:

Example 1:

If someone has multiple 2s (more than one) in their chart, there are very high chances of depression. Children born in this century have multiple 2s in their chart which is why depression cases are too frequent these days.

Example 2:

If someone's driver is 4 and the conductor is 2, or if the driver is 2 and the conductor is 4, this combination has a very high likelihood of leading to depression. This is because, in this combination, the Moon is in the company of Rahu. The Moon represents the queen, while Rahu can be likened to a gangster. The queen prefers to stay away from the gangster and tends to avoid interactions. She avoids talking to anyone and prefers living alone in her room. All these factors can contribute to this person experiencing depression.

If someone's personal year is 9 or personal year is Anti to your Driver. There is a very high chance of having a depression in the personal year. If your driver is 4 and your personal year is 2 and also multiple 2s in your chart, there are very high chances you will pass through a depression.

Example 3:

If someone has multiple 2s in their chart and also an anti-D-C combination (i.e. 1/8, 8/1, 2/8, 8/2, 3/6, 6/3) it is an induction towards depression.

The solution to depression charts:

We cannot improve and change the chart and D-C combination. But we can help them mentally and emotionally. Parents should spend as much time as possible with their children. Parents should talk to their children daily, ask them about their daily routines, go on vacations, and play with them.

Remedies are also very helpful in these cases. Gayatri Pendent and Crystal bracelets should be worn.

Chapter 3

Why Do You Frequently Fall Ill? Detect and Uplift Your Health Sector

"Numbers whisper the story of our vitality. Master the numeric language, and let health become a harmonious symphony in the composition of your life."

Many people occasionally report that many of their family members are always infected with a disease irrespective of their age group.

In this chapter, we will learn how we can deal with these diseases and what are the yogas and remedies to get rid of these diseases according to your date of birth.

First of all, we'll see which yogas of your date of birth are affecting your health.

Write your date of birth on paper. For example, I am writing a date of birth as 13/02/1967. Find out your driver and conductor number. The driver number is the sum of your date and the conductor number is the total of all numbers in your date of birth. According to this date of birth, the date is 13, so driver number is 1+ 3 equal to 4. When I sum all the digits of my date of birth, conductor number comes out as 2.

Now you have your birth date, year, and month and your driver and conductor number.

If your driver and conductor numbers are not compatible, if both numbers are opposite or anti to each other, you may face health issues.

For example, if your driver is 1, and the conductor is 8 or your driver is 8 and the conductor is 1. This is a powerful signal of health issues.

If your driver is 4 and the conductor is 9 or the conductor is 4 and the driver is 9, this is also the Yog of health issues.

If your driver is 2 and the conductor is 8 or the conductor is 2 and the driver is 8. This combination is also a sign of health issues.

If you have a driver conductor combination of two and six. It is a signal of health issues.

Multiple sevens in your chart are also responsible for health issues. If you have two or more than two sevens in your chat, you may be struggling with your health.

One side is your driver conductor combination and the other side is multiple 7s in your chart and the third side of health issues is the spelling of your name.

If your name spelling is anti or opposite to your driver or conductor (especially driver) there are higher chances of health issues.

For example: If your driver number is 8 and your name spelling is on 1. You may have poor health.

You can still face health issues even if your driver conductor combination is good, your name spelling is correct and you don't have multiple 7s in your chat.

The Vastu of your house can also affect your health. The primary health sector, according to the Vastu, is northeast. After this, East is also a health sector.

If you have stairs, a toilet, or a kitchen in the Northeast or East of your house. This is going to affect your health. If you have all these in the northeast or East of your house, this will affect children first. After children, the males and then the ladies of the house are affected.

We cannot change your date of birth, so your driver and conductor number remain unchanged. You can improve your health sector by correcting your name spelling.

If anyone in your house is struggling with major health problems, I am writing two remedies for this.

First: wear Gayatri pendent.

Chant Gayatri Mantra frequently in your house.

You can also play the audio of Gayatri Mantra.

Second: on Mondays and Wednesdays go to a Ganesh temple. Offer yellow clothes and a coin of 5 or 10 rupees to Lord Ganesh. Offer five laddus and give them to the Pandit or poor. And pray to resolve your health problems.

By doing all these remedies regularly, your health will improve. We will discuss the remedies according to Vastu in my next book.

CHAPTER 4
IDENTIFYING SPIRITUAL PROGRESS AND DIVINE CONNECTIONS THROUGH YOUR BIRTHDATE

"As numbers weave the fabric of our existence, delve into the secrets they hold for your health. Numerology isn't just math; it's the art of mastering well-being."

Can numerology guide if someone wants to go toward spirituality? Or can numerology tell us about our connection to god? Let's see in this chapter.

There are only two planets that suggest a spiritual journey or spiritual growth: Jupiter (3) and Ketu (7). Ketu holds greater significance than Jupiter, being a more powerful indicator of a spiritual journey, while Jupiter serves as a catalyst for spirituality. Even if you possess only the number 3, it can still influence you toward spirituality.

Keep in mind that the numbers 3 and 7 should be directly present in your date of birth (DOB) or in your chart as driver or conductor numbers. If these numbers are derived from the Kua number, there are fewer chances of the person experiencing spiritual inclinations.

There may be a conflict if you have 3 and 7 as well as number 6 in your chart. Because 3 and 7 want you to become spiritual and 6 want you to live a luxurious life.

Here is an example of DOB representing this case:

13-02-1967

	9	22
3		7
	11	66

D= 4

C= 2

K= 6

Chapter 5

ELEVATING YOUR WELLNESS, WEALTH, AND RELATIONSHIP DOMAINS

> *"In the tapestry of life, health is the golden thread. Let numerology be your guide, unraveling the secrets to master your well-being with every calculated digit."*

I believe that from his very first breath, a child gets involved in three things and at the end, he dies in these three things. We all are working and living only for these three things: health, money and relationships. People always ask about only these three aspects. So let's talk about them in this chapter.

Money and Career:

If you want to maintain money and a career throughout your life, you should focus on the north and west zones because the north is the zone of Kuber, and the west is the zone of Varun, who is the father of Goddess Laxmi. Don't place any junk in the north and west; keep the north always clean, and the kitchen and staircase should never be in the north.

Indirectly, S-E is connected to money because it is the zone of Venus, the zone of luxury and glamor. Therefore, for better utilization of money, keep this zone defect-free. If SE is defective, you cannot enjoy the benefits of your money; all your money will get spent on medical bills and some unnecessary things.

Health:

The zones of health are NE and East. Health zones are the master zones as they can affect other zones also because the source of the energy is the North-East. Defects in these zones can lead to head-related problems. Keep these zones clean, keep them open for air, and allow natural light coming from these zones. Also, avoid the staircase, toilet, and kitchen in these zones.

Relationship:

The zone of family relations is the East, and the zone of commercial relations is south and south-west. For better strength of the relationships, avoid any defect in these zones. Avoid any T-point underground water bodies in these zones. Build plantations in these zones.

There is also a fourth factor no one talks about. In my entire career, no one asked me about this factor. This factor is spiritualism. We are so busy in our daily routine that we never want to improve this factor. People want to gain first and then they think about worshiping. North-East and East are zones of spiritualism.

CHAPTER 6

NUMEROLOGY'S UNIVERSAL REMEDY: A MASTER SOLUTION FOR ALL CHALLENGES

"Numbers are the silent architects of our health. Master the language of numerology, and sculpt a foundation of well-being that echoes through the corridors of your life."

We always talk about remedies whenever there is a defect or weak point in our date of birth. In this chapter, we are going to talk about the 'master solution' which is different from remedies.

This solution works even when remedies cannot do anything. Whenever you are confused about what to do, whenever things are not in your control, whenever you are about to give up, just delve under the shade of Lord Ganesh.

On Mondays or Wednesdays, offer bundi or besan laddus (sweet delicacies), a 1.25-meter-long yellow scarf, and a modest 5 or 10 rupee coin to Lord Ganesh. Also, pray to Lord Ganesh to solve your problem. Close your eyes, think about Lord Ganesh, and imagine that your problem is getting solved.

Imagine yourself living happily without that problem. When this image is made in your mind, thank Lord Ganesh. Remember that prayers have more power than any solution.

Meanings:

Bundi–

- A granule of gram flour that has been passed through a sieve and fried.

- A sweetmeat-ball made from these granules.

Besan laddus – Gram flour laddoo, is a round-shaped Indian dessert made from gram flour, sugar, ghee, and nuts.

MAY I ASK YOU FOR A SMALL FAVOR?

I want to express my sincere gratitude for choosing to invest your time in reading this book. Your decision to explore this work among countless others means a lot to me.

I hope that within these pages, you've discovered actionable insights that can enhance your daily life. Your journey doesn't have to end here, though.

May I kindly request an additional 30 seconds of your valuable time?

Sharing your thoughts about the book through a review would be immensely appreciated. Your review serves as a beacon, guiding other readers to take a chance on my books. It's a small gesture that carries significant weight in the world of authors.

To submit your review effortlessly, please **Scan** the **QR Code** below. It will take you directly to the book's review page:

"Master Your HEALTH With Numerology"

Alternatively, you can also find the "**Reviews Section**" of this book's page on Amazon.

Your review will require just a minute of your time but will make a monumental difference in helping me connect with a broader audience and I eagerly look forward to reading your review.

Once again, thank you for your unwavering support of my work.

CHAPTER 7

THE SIGNIFICANCE OF FEBRUARY 5TH: COMMENCEMENT OF THE PERSONAL YEAR

*"Numerology – the silent healer.
Uncover the secrets within the digits,
master your health, and let the
arithmetic of well-being guide you
towards a healthier, harmonious life."*

In this chapter, we will learn about personal days, months, and years, how they are useful to us, and how we can calculate them.

Personal years, months, and days help us navigate our lives, improve our decision-making, and enable us to plan for our future. If you wish to take risks or achieve something significant in your life, you must make the right decisions at the right time; otherwise, you might fail. That's why personal years, months, and days play a crucial role.

For example, let's consider a date of birth (DOB) of 13-02-1967. The driver for this DOB is 4, and the conductor is 2. I will perform all the calculations for the year 2023. However, you can use this method on any date you choose.

Now, I want to know how 2023 will be for me.

Calculating Personal Year:

1. Write your DOB, but instead of writing your actual year of birth, write the year for which you want to calculate your personal year number. If your DOB is 13-02-1967 and you want to check for the year 2023, you need to write your date like this- 13-02-2023.

2. Calculator all digits until you have a single-digit number. This single-digit number will be your personal year. For this example, it is 4.

3. Now compare this personal year number with your driver number. If it's a good match this year will be good for you,

If you want to calculate for 2023, you need to write your date of birth (DOB), but instead of writing the year of birth, you will write 2023. So, the date will look like this: 13-02-2023. Now, add all the digits of this date until you have a single-digit number. 1 + 3 + 0 + 2 + 2 + 0 + 2 + 3 equals 13, which further reduces to 4. This number (4) is the personal year number for this DOB in 2023. When calculating the personal year number, we only consider the Driver number; the Conductor number is not taken into account.

The personal year number for this DOB in 2023 comes out as 4, which corresponds to the number of Rahu. It can be said that Rahu will be in conjunction with the Driver for the entire year 2023. This is only a temporary relationship lasting one year. In this case, you can say that Rahu is aligning with Rahu because both the personal year number for 2023 and the Driver number are 4. Since 4 is compatible with 4, 2023 is likely to be a good year for this person. They can take risks and start something they may have been planning for many years, with very high chances of success.

Calculation of personal month:

Now, I want to determine how OCTOBER 2023 will be for this DOB. October is the 10th month of the year, and the total of 10 is 1 + 0 = 1. After this, we need to add our personal year number to this month's number to calculate our personal month number. In this example, the personal year number was 4; therefore, the personal month number for October will be 1 + 4 = 5. Now, we will check its relationship with the Driver number.

If it is a good combination, you can make good and important decisions this month. However, if this number is contradictory or uncomfortable with your Driver number, you should avoid making significant life decisions in that month.

Calculation of personal day:

Now, I want to check for a specific day. I want to know how October 15, 2023, will be for me. First of all, we need to calculate the total for the day of the date. To do this, we simply add all the digits until we have a single-digit number. So, for the mentioned date, the day total will be 1 + 5 + 1 + 0 + 2 + 0 + 2 + 3 = 14, which further reduces to 5.

From the previous example, the personal year number was 4, the personal month for October was 5, and the day total for this particular date came out as 5. Now, we need to add all three of these to obtain our personal day number. Therefore, 4 + 5 + 5 equals 14, which further reduces to 5. That's how our personal day number is calculated as 5.

If this number is comfortable with the driver, you can make important decisions on this particular day, otherwise, you should avoid taking important steps on this particular day.

Starting off a personal year:

A new year starts from the first of January, but a personal year starts from the 5th of February. In our example, the personal year number for 2023 was 4. It means 4 will affect this person from 5th Feb 2023 to 5th Feb 2024.

The crucial factor is the personal year; the entire year will operate in accordance with the personal year number. Yes, it can be influenced by the personal month and personal day, but, in general, it will be mainly affected by the personal year. However, if you are about to make any important decisions, you should consider both the personal year and the personal month, along with the personal day, for the best results.

If you have the option to choose a date (perhaps for surgery, a meeting, or an interview), you can select the optimal date with the assistance of the personal day number.

CHAPTER 8
ADJUSTING FATE: REMEDIES FOR CHANGES IN PERSONAL YEAR

"In the world of digits, health is the prime equation. Master your health with the precision of numerology, where each number is a step towards a healthier, happier you."

We select remedies based on our date of birth (DOB) and astrological chart. Some may wonder if their personal year changes annually, leading to the question of whether remedies should be adjusted every year. However, this is not accurate; there is no need to change your remedies with each passing year.

Suppose you were following the remedies of Venus and your personal year came out on number 3. Now the remedy you were doing and your personal year are enemies to each other. But don't worry, a personal year number tells us about the behavior of that particular year for us. It doesn't affect our chart and remedies. Remedies are based on our requirements and missing numbers. They have no relation with the personal year.

Another reason for not changing the remedies is that the relationship of the personal year with our driver number is a temporary relationship. And temporary relations have no significant impact on our fortune.

If you keep changing your remedies again and again, they will be no longer effective.

Here is one thing we need to care about: that if our personal year is either 9 or anti to our driver, we will acquire Gayatri Pendent for that period. Gayatri Pendent will help us manage this period and there is no need to change the remedies.

Chapter 9

A Deep Dive Into Direct and Indirect Solutions

"In the numeric symphony of life, health is the melody. Master your health with the precision of numerology, where every note resonates with well-being."

In this chapter, we will talk about direct and indirect remedies and the difference between them.

Let's understand with some examples:

Example A:

Let's assume a DOB is 13-02-1967. The chart is below-

4	9	22
3		7
	11	66

D= 4

C= 2

K= 6

You can see that the driver and conductor are 'opposite' numbers in this example. Whenever we are choosing 'direct' remedies, first we need to choose remedies for the driver and then for the conductor. But the condition is that the D-C combination should not be 'anti'. When the combination is 'neutral' or 'friend' we need to do the remedies of both driver and conductor. But if this is an opposite combination, then avoiding the remedies is a better choice.

Therefore, in this example, we cannot do the remedies of numbers 4 and 2. Now let's look at the birth chart. Because numbers 5 and 8 are missing in this chart, this person should do the remedies of these two numbers. But one thing should be taken care of the missing number should not be anti or opposite to the driver. This person can do the direct remedies of number 5 but he should avoid the remedies of number 8 because it's not compatible with the driver.

In this case, we have to follow the indirect remedies of number 8 to fulfill its absence.

Example B:

Assume a DOB is 19-02-1995. The chart will look like this-

	999	
	55	
8	1111	

D= 1
C= 8
K= 5

In this example, D-C combination is anti. This person can not perform the 'direct' remedies of driver and conductor. 2, 4, 3, 7, and 6 are missing in this chart. Now number 4 is compatible with the driver, but not with the conductor. Therefore, we should do indirect remedies for the number 4.

Number 3 is a friend with both the sun and Saturn. therefore direct remedies of both driver and conductor can be followed. Number 2 is compatible with the driver but not with the conductor. Therefore, indirect remedies are applicable. Number 7 is neutral with every number but because the remedies of number 7 are exactly similar to the remedies of number 4, and we are avoiding the direct remedies of number 4 therefore we also have to avoid the direct remedies of number 7, in this case, indirect remedies are a better choice for the fulfillment of missing number 7. Number 6 is a friend of both the driver and conductor which is why direct remedies can be performed for missing 6. But we need to be careful here, as you can see that direct remedies for number 3 and number 6 are allowed in this example but these two numbers are enemies to each other therefore we cannot perform direct remedies for both numbers, we have to select one number. The better option is to do the direct remedies for number 6 and indirect remedies for number 3 because today's era is the era of Venus, the era of luxury, glamor, and money. Venus fits perfectly in today's world therefore, remedies of Venus are more important to us. But according to your need, you can go with direct remedies of number 3.

Example C:

A DOB is 15-07-1986. And here is the chart-

	9	
	55	7
8	111	66

D= 6

C= 1

K= 5

D-C combination is a friend combination in this example. Therefore, direct remedies of both driver and conductor can be done. Here numbers 4, 3, and 2 are missing. Number 4 is compatible with the driver and neutral with conduct. Therefore, we can do direct remedies for this number. Number 3 is the enemy of 6 therefore, we can only follow indirect remedies. Number 2 is neutral with the driver and friend with the Conductor, therefore, direct remedies can be performed. That's how you can choose between direct and indirect remedies for missing numbers.

Remember that there is no importance of Kua number in the remedies. You don't need to care about Kua while you are selecting the remedies.

Here are Indirect Remedies for missing numbers:

4, 3 = remedies of wood element

8, 2, 5= wear crystal bracelet

9= Red Tilak on the forehead and can wear Red thread on the wrist

1= Offer water to the Sun (when the driver or conductor is not 8), drink more and more water

7= wear golden and silver metal strap watches

6= wear only golden and metal strap watches

Chapter 10
Numerology's Insight into Children's Social Circles: Identifying Risks

"Numbers are the compass guiding us through the labyrinth of health. Master the numerological map, and let it lead you to the pinnacle of well-being."

Many parents are concerned about their children getting indulged in bad company. By looking into a child's DOB, let's figure out the chance of his/her getting indulged in bad company. We can also check if the child would be obedient or not.

Numbers for Bad Company:

- Numbers 4, 2, and 8 are responsible for indulging in bad company. We are not saying that a person with these numbers will surely get indulged in bad company, but there are changes if the environment is familiar with this.

- These three numbers can propel a thought of indulging in a bad company.

- If the DC combination is 6-6 or 4-8 or 4-4 or 1-1 there are chances of involvement in bad company.

Number of Obedience:

- Only number 6 is responsible for obedience. If a child has number 6 in the birth chart, there is a very high chance that he/she will be obedient. But 6 should not come from the Kua number. All these things depend on the child's environment, so we should also provide the child with a good environment.

- If 6 is absent, its complimentary number 5 can be responsible for the child's obedience.

CHAPTER 11

NAVIGATING TIME: CHOOSING THE RIGHT WRIST COMPANION

"Numerology is the language of wellness. Decode the numbers, unravel the patterns, and master your health – a journey written in the arithmetic of vitality."

Should we wear wrist watches? What types of wrist watches should we wear? What are the benefits of wearing them? And are there any negative consequences to not wearing a watch? What is the principal? What is the logic and sciences behind wrist watches? Let's understand these questions in this chapter.

We stopped wearing watches as we started carrying mobile phones. Everyone should wear a wristwatch because, in terms of numerology, it is very beneficial for our fortune. These are points we should care about while wearing a wristwatch:

- Mostly wristwatches are worn on the left hand, but there is no problem wearing it on the right hand.

- Avoid leather and rubber strap watches; a metal strap/chain watch is preferable.

- The color of the chain/strap should be golden or a mix of golden and silver, but avoid wearing a silver color alone.

A watch is considered a living thing because it has an energy source and so many moving parts in it. We should avoid leather and rubber straps because these materials are insulating and prevent the energy from transferring into our body. A metal strap allows this energy into our body, increasing our energy level and improving our opportunity and relationship sectors.

Chapter 12

Choosing the Right Pendant: A Guide for Challenging Birth Dates

"Your health, a numerical masterpiece waiting to be unveiled. In the world of numerology, discover the brushstrokes that paint the canvas of well-being."

Many times, we have to face some tricky DOBs; these tricky dates of birth can confuse us, resulting in incorrect calculations. In this chapter, we will look at these types of cases.

Example 1:

Assume a DOB of a female is 14-03-1984.

44	9	
33	5	
88	11	

D= 5

C= 3

K= 8

Now, because the number 6 is absent from the chart, the first thing that comes to our mind is to suggest the Pyra Pendent. However, when either the driver or conductor is 3, we cannot use Pyra because the total of Pyra is on number 6, which is the enemy of number 3.

Now, you might think that Sun-Pyra should be the best pendent, but this is also a disaster. The best-fit Pendent/Yantra, for this example, is the Sun (Surya).

Example 2:

A DOB of a male is 23-02-1990.

MASTER YOUR HEALTH WITH NUMEROLOGY

	99	22
3	5	
8	11	

D= 5

C= 8

K= 1

Now, number 6 is missing from this chart, so you might think that Pyra and Surya are the recruits for this chart. Therefore, this person should wear the Sun-Pyra pendent. Pyra should be worn in this example, but this person must avoid the Sun because the conductor is 8. If either the driver or conductor is 8, we must avoid the Sun Pendent. Only Pyra alone is the best pendent for this date of birth.

Example 3:

Imaging a DOB of a female is 11-01-1971

	9	2
3		7
	1111	

D= 2

C= 3

Now, both numbers 5 and 6 are absent here, so you might think that Budh-Pyra should be given to this person. However, because the conductor is number 3, this person cannot wear Pyra. The pendent this person should wear in this example is Surya-Budh.

Some important points about pendents are:

- Because yantras are comprise up of silver, they become blackish because of corrosion. If a Pendent becomes black, its power is almost nil. In that case, ensure that your yantra is always silver, and keep cleaning it from time to time.

- A Pendent is to be worn by only one person. You cannot wear a yantra if it was already worn by someone else. The Pendent you are going to wear should be fresh and new. Because after wearing yantras you get connected to our energy, and because everyone's energy is different, you cannot wear used yantras.

- Pendents are always made in triangular shape because this is the shape of a pyramid in 2D. Pyramids are responsible for enhancing the power of your energy and they are also responsible for balancing the energy.

Role of Yanta vs Gemstone

In this chapter, we will learn about the role of pendents and bracelets we are given to wear.

Many people believe in gemstones and prefer to wear them as lockets and rings. Gemstones are expensive, that's why they look important and useful to us. But I never prefer gemstones because, in our ancient shastra, there is no mention of gemstones for the purpose of numerology. People used to wear gemstones as an ornament for showing off. Only to make a profit out of it they connected it with the occult. I will suggest no one use gemstones because they are unaffordable to the common man and the authenticity is also questionable.

Remedies should be easy and affordable so that the Pendents are the best choice. All the pendents are

Authentic and suggested by our shastras (except-pyra). Pendents are pure because they are made up of pure silver metal. You can also feel the power of Pendents when they are energized, while this is not possible with gemstones.

Bracelets are also a good choice because they are effective and easy to use. We can select the bracelets according to our needs and missing numbers.

CONCLUSION

Congratulations on reaching the culmination of this book. Your commitment to reading through these pages signifies your dedication to personal growth and a thirst for knowledge. Completing a book is a remarkable achievement, and you should take a moment to acknowledge your accomplishment.

Throughout this journey, the aim has been to guide you toward shaping a destiny defined by success and fulfillment. Your investment in this book reflects a deep commitment to self-improvement, and for that, you should feel proud.

As you conclude this book, I trust that it has left you with valuable insights and a sense of empowerment. The road to a prosperous destiny is not always linear or without its challenges, but your newfound knowledge in smart questioning equips you to navigate these paths with confidence.

I genuinely hope that your voyage through these chapters has been both enlightening and engaging. The pursuit of a splendid life brimming with happiness and fulfillment is a commendable one, and your proactive steps toward this aspiration are evident through your persistence in reading this book. In the pursuit of success and a life well-lived, remember that knowledge is your most potent tool. With this, you hold the key to unlocking the limitless potential within you.

As you close this final page and embark on the journey that follows, I extend my heartfelt best wishes for a future filled with accomplishments and contentment.

Cheers,
Sooraj Achar

MAY I ASK YOU FOR A SMALL FAVOR?

I want to express my sincere gratitude for choosing to invest your time in reading this book. Your decision to explore this work among countless others means a lot to me.

I hope that within these pages, you've discovered actionable insights that can enhance your daily life. Your journey doesn't have to end here, though.

May I kindly request an additional 30 seconds of your valuable time?

Sharing your thoughts about the book through a review would be immensely appreciated. Your review serves as a beacon, guiding other readers to take a chance on my books. It's a small gesture that carries significant weight in the world of authors.

To submit your review effortlessly, please **Scan** the **QR Code** below. It will take you directly to the book's review page:

"Master Your HEALTH With Numerology"

Alternatively, you can also find the "**Reviews Section**" of this book's page on Amazon.

Your review will require just a minute of your time but will make a monumental difference in helping me connect with a broader audience and I eagerly look forward to reading your review.

Once again, thank you for your unwavering support of my work.

PREVIEW OF MY NEXT BOOK IN THE SERIES

Master Your MONEY With Numerology

Establish Wealth With Numerical Intelligence, Unlock Financial Fortune, Conquer Hidden Obstacles, and Achieve Lasting Prosperity

This book is Numerology Professional Success Guide, where you get to learn the advanced level of numerology application and implementation to transform your life towards a happier destiny.

Below is the list of Important Topics to be covered in the Upcoming Book in the Numerology Series:

1. How To Detect Money Sector?

2. Common Factor Among Rich & Successful People

3. Power Of Number 6: Venus

4. Unlocking The Future: Predictions Beyond The Date Of Birth

5. Jackpot: Big Arrows And Small Arrows

6. A Guide To House Numbers & Remedial Measures

7. Home Sweet Goals: When And How You'll Own?

8. Decode Your Car's Energy: Numerology Tips And Remedies

9. Sell Your Unsold Properties Using Numerology

10. Karmic Debts Of Previous Birth !!

11. Numerology For Stock Market

12. Top-5 Tips & Tricks In Numerology

Stay Tuned to explore all the series of **Self-Help** Books coming up !!

PREVIEW OF MY BEST SELLING BOOKS

Series-1: Master Your Life with NUMEROLOGY

★ **Why do 80% of People Fail to Recognize their True Potential ??**

These self-help books will help you **Recognize, Transform, and Navigate** your life toward a **Happier Destiny**.

I always say that your **Date of Birth** is so precious. God has placed many diamonds on your date of birth that you are not aware of. It doesn't matter if your date of birth is good or bad. The idea is how you can take the best out of your date of birth.

Master Your DESTINY With Numerology is a perfect, **complete beginner's guide** for those who are new to numerology.

★ What Role Does Numerology Play in Your Life?

- You have been surrounded by numbers since the day you were Born. Now use them to unlock your Destiny.

- Wherever you go in your life, the numbers always move on with you.

- When you are born, on the very first day of your life, you get your date of birth, which is made up of numbers.

- When you get admitted to school, you get your roll number.

- When you get your results, you get a percentage of numbers.

- When you get a job, you get a salary and EMP-ID number.

- When you buy any vehicle, it has a number plate.

- When you travel, you get a ticket and seat number

- When you check into a hotel, you get a room number.

- When you want to call a person, you have to dial numbers.

- When you get married, there is also a date attached to it.

- If there is Life, there are Numbers. You cannot get rid of Numbers.

★ Your **Name Spelling** also plays an important role according to your date of birth. Believe me or not, **30% to 40%** of your success or failure depends on your name spelling. If you keep your name spelling correct, you can achieve 30% to 40% more success in your life.

♥ **Master Your DESTINY With Numerology will help you...**

✓ Recognize Your Strengths and Weaknesses.

✓ Find Your Lucky Numbers and Colors.

✓ Correct Your Name Spelling without changing your documents.

✓ Choose the Right Profession.

✓ Find a Compatible Life-Partner.

✓ With Simple Remedies for All Your Problems.

✓ Check Your Foreign or Abroad Opportunities.

✓ Predict your Future Years, Months, and Days of importance, which helps you make Better Decisions.

✓ Understand the Behavioral Patterns of People Around You.

✓ Transform and Navigate your life for a Better Future.

★ If you are ready to make a commitment to yourself that you want to learn everything that is presented to you, then it is our commitment to you that this will surely help you a lot. There is no reason why this book will not change your destiny or transform your future. But, there is an important thing you must keep in mind, i.e., **"You will bring this change through TRANSFORMATION, not through MIRACLES"**.

★ If you learn **Numerology**, then

(a) "You will be **awakened**", which makes it likely to "**transform**" your life.

(b) Ultimately, "You will be able to **navigate** your life".

★ Life is all about "**Awakening**,", "**Transformation**," and eventually, "Knowing How To **Navigate** It?"

★ Order **Master Your DESTINY With Numerology** now to make the most of your

Health, Relationships, Career, and Money by unlocking the **Power of Numbers**.

Check Out My Best Selling Books Here:

1. Master Your DESTINY With Numerology

2. Master Your NAME-SPELLING With Numerology

3. Master Your RELATIONSHIPS With Numerology

4. Master Your MONEY With Numerology

5. Master Your HEALTH With Numerology

6. Master Your PROFESSIONAL GOALS With Numerology

Series-2: Master Your Life with VASTU

★ How Can These Books Work Miracles in Your Life?

This Self-Help Book is A Perfect Blueprint Describing Ancient Principles for Modern Living. A Step-by-step Practical Guide for Beginners to Creating a Positive Living Space and for Optimal Well-Being.

Learn:

★ How to Implement Feng-Shui/Vastu in your Day-to-Day Life !!

★ What Role Do Feng-Shui and Vastu Play in Your Life?

★ Relationship between Vastu and Feng-Shui?

Vastu is used to Diagnose, and Feng Shui is the Remedy. Vastu is used to identify the disease, and Feng Shui is the medicine. Vastu and Feng Shui are complementary to each other.

Vastu Shastra is an Ancient Indian Science of architecture and construction, which is based on the principles of harmony and balance between humans and their environment. The main focus of Vastu is to create a harmonious balance between the 5-Elements of nature, i.e., Earth, Water, Air, Fire, & Space. It emphasizes directions and orientation and uses various elements like colors, shapes, and materials to create a balance and positive energy in the living spaces.

Feng Shui, on the other hand, is a Chinese Philosophical System of harmonizing everyone with the surrounding environment. It is based on the principles of Qi (Chi), the life force that flows through all living things, and Yin and Yang, the balance of opposite forces. Feng Shui focuses on the placement of objects, furniture, and structures in living spaces to optimize the flow of energy, or "Qi." It also considers the orientation of the building, the placement of doors and windows, and the use of colors, shapes, & materials to create balance & harmony.

In summary, both Vastu and Feng Shui aim to create balance and harmony in living spaces, but Vastu is more focused on directions and orientation, while Feng Shui emphasizes the flow of energy & balance of opposing forces.

★ The Benefits of Reading This Book Include:

✓ **Health and Well-Being:** Vastu principles aim to create a harmonious and balanced environment that can promote physical, mental, and emotional well-being.

✓ **Financial Prosperity:** Vastu principles are believed to help attract positive energy and good fortune, leading to financial prosperity.

✓ **Improved Relationships:** Vastu principles can help create an atmosphere of peace and harmony, which can lead to improved relationships with family, friends, & colleagues.

✓ **Increased Productivity:** A Vastu-compliant environment is said to be conducive to productivity and efficiency, leading to greater success in personal & professional life.

✓ **Spiritual Growth:** Vastu principles are based on ancient Vedic knowledge and aim to promote spiritual growth & enlightenment.

✓ **Enhanced Creativity:** Vastu principles are believed to enhance creativity and inspiration, which can be beneficial for artists, writers, & other creative professionals.

✓ **Better Sleep Quality:** Vastu principles can help create a peaceful and relaxing environment, which can improve the quality of sleep and help reduce stress & anxiety.

✓ **Improved Mental Clarity:** A Vastu-compliant environment is said to help clear the mind and improve mental clarity, which can be beneficial for decision-making & problem-solving.

✓ **Enhanced Career Prospects:** Vastu principles can help align one's career goals with their personal strengths and abilities, leading to greater career success & satisfaction.

★ Overall, the benefits of Vastu can contribute to a more Balanced, Harmonious, & Fulfilling Life.

★ Order "Master Your DESTINY With Vastu" now to make the most of your Health, Relationships, Career, & Money by unlocking the Power of Directions.

Check Out My Best Selling Books Here:

1. Master Your DESTINY With Vastu

2. Master Your GROWTH With Vastu

3. Master Your WEALTH With Vastu

4. Master Your CAREER With Vastu

Series-3: The Ultimate Self-Healing Mastery Series

"**The Art of Balancing Yin-Yang Energy**" is an enlightening and transformative guide that unveils the ancient wisdom of harmonizing the opposing forces of Yin and Yang within ourselves and the world around us. Drawing from the profound teachings of Eastern philosophy and modern-day practices, this book offers a comprehensive understanding of Yin and Yang and provides practical techniques to achieve balance, harmony, and fulfillment in all aspects of life.

In today's fast-paced and chaotic world, finding balance is more crucial than ever. Whether you seek to improve your relationships, enhance your well-being, or achieve success in your career, understanding and aligning the Yin-Yang energy within you can be a game-changer. This book takes you on a transformative journey, guiding you through the principles, practices, and benefits of embracing the art of balancing Yin-Yang energy.

By delving into the core concepts of Yin and Yang, you will gain insights into their dynamic interplay and learn how to identify and rectify imbalances in your life. Discover how the complementary forces of Yin and Yang manifest in various aspects, such as work-life balance, emotional well-being, and personal growth. With this knowledge, you can cultivate harmony and create a fulfilling and purpose-driven life.

★ Here are the Top-15 Benefits:

1. Harmony and Balance: Balancing yin-yang energy promotes a sense of harmony and balance within oneself and in relationships with others.

2. Enhanced Well-being: Balanced yin-yang energy contributes to overall physical, mental, and emotional well-being.

3. Stress Reduction: Maintaining balanced yin-yang energy helps reduce stress and promotes a state of calmness and relaxation.

4. Increased Energy: Balancing yin-yang energy enhances vitality and boosts energy levels.

5. Emotional Stability: Harmonizing yin-yang energy supports emotional stability, reducing mood swings and promoting emotional resilience.

6. Improved Focus and Clarity: Balanced yin-yang energy enhances mental clarity, concentration, and focus.

7. Better Decision-Making: When yin-yang energy is in equilibrium, it fosters better decision-making skills and promotes sound judgment.

8. Enhanced Intuition: Balancing yin-yang energy can amplify intuition and inner wisdom.

9. Improved Relationships: Harmonizing yin-yang energy cultivates healthier and more balanced relationships, promoting understanding and cooperation.

10. Greater Creativity: Balanced yin-yang energy can enhance creativity and innovation in various aspects of life.

11. Physical Healing: Balancing yin-yang energy supports the body's natural healing abilities and can contribute to faster recovery from illnesses or injuries.

12. Emotional Healing: Harmonizing yin-yang energy aids in emotional healing and facilitates the release of emotional blockages.

13. Enhanced Digestion: Balanced yin-yang energy promotes optimal digestion and helps alleviate digestive issues.

14. Hormonal Balance: Balancing yin-yang energy can help regulate hormonal imbalances and improve overall hormonal health.

15. Improved Sleep Quality: Harmonized yin-yang energy promotes better sleep quality and can help alleviate sleep disorders.

Check Out My Best Selling Books Here:

1. The Art of Balancing YIN-YANG Energy

2. The 7 Energy Needs

3. Discover Your Life Purpose

4. The Power Of ONE Question

5. The Fear of Death

TESTIMONIALS

These are a few feedbacks from my clients across different parts of the world. Kindly go through their reviews to understand how Numerology and Vastu helped them.

1. Ekta Gupta – Kolkata, India

"2021 is a difficult year for me. I have consulted a few numerologists. I have received vague answers and complicated solutions. I'm new to numerology. Charges were expensive. Sooraj is a good and kind soul. He is very patient with me. He answered all my questions. I had 1000 questions. More ever he helped me to find a business name with no extra

charges. I'm grateful to him. With your help, I'm sorted out with my business name. I had a lot of anxiety about it. I'm confident now. Sooraj is a helpful soul. He is patient and explains if one has questions. He doesn't rush into closing the job. You can consult him easily. I am going to recommend him to newbies like me. He is not going to cheat you or misguide you".

2. Neetu Ganglani - Stanley, Hongkong

"Hello Sooraj, I can't thank you enough. At the age of 45, I could find an ideal life partner for myself. And my compatibility with the boy I like. Got to know our strengths and weaknesses. Your suggestions helped me to find the right life partner. You have a bright future. Good luck"

3. R Lensly Kwaimani - Solomon Islands, Oceania

"Dear friend, glad I came across you. My daughter Felinda Kwaimani is sick for a long time and I was very much worried. Thank you for giving suggestions and guidance".

4. Seham Shabhir - Talagang, Pakistan

"You're one of the best numerologists...your predictions are correct...you are a very humble person...you gave answers to all of my questions in detail ... I'm very thankful to you. Ur remedies prove very helpful for me. He is the very best numerologist... I recommend him for all.. u should consult him to get rid of your problems..his remedies work like a magic"

5. Naveen Kumar - Bengaluru, India

"Sooraj is a gem as a human and as a professional. Before approaching Sooraj, I have enquired and got inputs from other numerologists and I did some research as well. I Was not satisfied with the answers provided by them and most of them were behind fees, even after paying for the consultation they charge extra for clarifying doubts. However, Sooraj was awesome in client satisfaction and the way he follows up with the client for providing suggestions. He takes the initiative to follow up and provide the best solutions and describes the reason for the input. I definitely suggest Sooraj to anyone who is looking for start-up business names or anything related to numerology. He has a good amount of knowledge and patience to answer all my queries".

6. Sneha S - Karnataka, India

"Hi Sooraj, it's a great prediction starting from Personality Traits to our Abroad Opportunities to future achievements. Everything is perfectly predicted with correct proof and explanations which help us to understand our lives better and take steps accordingly to numerology. Everyone are curious to know more about their life just to know when, how & what situations they will come across and how they need to overcome everything. Thanks a lot, Sooraj, for the best Numerology Prediction which helped us to understand ourselves better".

7. Aditya S - Mumbai, India

"Sooraj, your numerology predictions are brilliant and accurate. Your Suggestions

helped me find out whether my current job is suitable for me or not. I would suggest people consult you in due course of time".

8. M Nabanita - West Bengal, India

"Hi Sooraj, it's helpful and gives me a quick idea and help. Thank you so much for being there. It helped me to understand my situation It helps in my career and marriage. The information is good".

9. Naresh Kumar – Bangalore, India

"Hello Sooraj, it was satisfactory. Can decide further based on the info shared & also can see positive outcomes looking forward to checking how it works".

10. Harishchandra Dnyaneshwar Deshmukh – Delhi, India

"Hi sir, Padhai puri nahi kar paya, 11 k salary he, Stable nahi hu life me, Business success nahi milta. Thank u sir for sharing my report and helping me understand my strengths and weaknesses".

AUTHOR PROFILE

Follow **Author's Profile Page** to get updates on all his books: **https://amazon.com/author/sooraj_achar**

Grab your **Free Gift** if you missed it: **https://gift.sooraj-achar.com/**

Please Leave Your **Valuable Review** here: **Master Your HEALTH With Vastu**

For 1-to-1 consultation, scan the **QR code** or contact: **connect@sooraj-achar.com**

Follow the **Author's BookBub** Profile: **BookBub Author Profile**

Stay Connected to the **Author's Social Media Handles** below

https://amzn.to/3CgQHF9

https://medium.com/@soorajachar99

https://bit.ly/3M7gIu2

instagram.com/psychology_of_numberz/

https://bit.ly/3dO6aDh

https://bit.ly/3LXBTyz

https://bit.ly/3E9vKxc

DISCLAIMER

This book is for educational purposes only. Readers acknowledge that the author does not render legal, financial, medical, or professional advice. The content within this book has been derived from various sources. Please consult a licensed professional before attempting any techniques outlined in this book.

By reading this document, the reader agrees that under no circumstances is the author responsible for any direct or indirect losses incurred as a result of the use of the information contained within this document, including but not limited to errors, omissions, or inaccuracies.

Adherence to all applicable laws and regulations, including international, federal, state, and local governing professional licensing, business practices, advertising, and all other jurisdictions, is the sole responsibility of the purchaser or reader.

Neither the author nor the publisher assumes any responsibility or liability whatsoever on behalf of the purchaser or reader of these materials. Any perceived slight of any individual or organization is purely unintentional.